STORY

Annette Fluker

authorHOUSE®

AuthorHouse™
1663 Liberty Drive
Bloomington, IN 47403
www.authorhouse.com
Phone: 1 (800) 839-8640

Published by AuthorHouse 02/28/2017

ISBN: 978-1-5246-5532-7 (sc)
ISBN: 978-1-5246-5531-0 (e)

Print information available on the last page.

This book is printed on acid-free paper.

KhAliA NAYA'DAH She Do what she
WANT-A you Better Leave Her alone
She Got A Father name David
A Mother NAME NeTT
A sister NAme SAMONE

A Brother Name	MAN Man

HE Plays	iNA BAND

A	Doggie with A BoNE

A Friend Name	RitA

THAt Know's How to treat Her

THEY Really GEt's ALONE

KHALiA NAYADAH | THere's,A Lot

ABOut HER | She reALLY Get's it oN

BY. annette
Fluker

Part one

Mom: Khalia!

Khalia: Yes Mom

Mom: You gonna be late for school

(8:10 Khalia is still sleep while sitting on the toilet)

(As Mom return's back to the bathroom)

Mom: Khalia

Khalia: Ok Mom, I'm almost all wash up!

Mom: All Khalia let me brush your hair, while you brush your teeth and wash up.

(15 minutes later)

Mom:

Mom: Let's go Khalia

(She makes it to school on time)

(Mom getting things done around the house while clear of David and the kids)

3:30 as Mom drive's to school to pick up Khalia

Khalia run's to the car, hop's right in

Khaia can I have a dollar Mom

(Off we go to for snacks and a small ride)

Khalia love;'s to take small ride's after school)

5:00 (Khalia is doing her homework)

Mom: Dinner time!

Dog: Ruff-Ruff-Ruff-Ruff-Ruff

Kid's what's for dinner

6:00 Very quiet the house become, cause Khalia enjoy's

Mom: Khalia, it's time for bed

Khalia: Ok Mom

Khalia gets a Kitten

(Saturday 7 am)

Khalia- Mom!

(As Mom tries to get some rest)

Mom- Yes Khalia

Khalia: Mom I want me some pancakes and syrup

Mom: Oh Khalia

(as mom say to herself, why not some cereal and milk)

Mom: Come Khalia let's go out to do some shopping.

Khalia: mom I don't wanna go shopping, I wanna go over Rita's house

Mom: No Khalia! Let's drop man man off to practice and someone off to the hair dresser.

(ruff-ruff-ruff)

Mom: no Chebocka, you must stay home out the door we went.

(as all the kid's were off, Khalia get's to play with Rita)

For a little while as mom pick's up David and shop, and then stop's by her sister Lucy's house.

Mom: Hello Lucy as we sat down and talk a while

Lucy: David do you think Khlaia would like a kitten

Mom: Oh what a pretty kitten

David: Yes, I think Khalia would like a kitten

(Mom and Dad get's home later with the kitten)

Dad: Khalia! Yell's out David

Khalia: Yes Dad!

Dad: Look Khalia we have you something special

(Khalia loved suprizes)

As dad shows her the kitten, she takes the kitten and off she runs into the room, as we follow her

Mom-Dad- what would you like to name her?

Khalia: Moo-Moo-she answered!

(Later as Mom and Dad sleeps)

4:00 am zzzzzzzzzzzzzzzzzzzzzzzzzzzzzzzzzzzzzzzzzzzzzzzzzzzzz

Khalia: Mommy, Mommy

Mom: Yes Khalia

Khalia: take this Kitty

(Mom turning over in bed)

Khlia: Mommy, Mommy

Mom: Yes Khalia?

(As Mom opens her eyes)

Khalia: Take this Kitty

(As Mom raises up)

Mom: What's wrong Khalia?

What's wrong with Moo-Moo?

Khalia: I don't want her

Mom: But why? Don't you like her?

Khalia: No! she cry too much

I can't get enough sleep!

Take Moo-moo

(As she cries)

Khalia: Take Moo-Moo back home.

Khalia has a Dream

David: Honey! Close the door, and have Khalia come inside, were going to have a bad storm.

Mom: come inside Khalia and have some lunch, put your toys in your toy box dear, were going to have a rain storm

(Khalia gathers her toys together and runs inside to prepare for a nice bowl of soup. Twenty minutes later fast a sleep she is as mom puts her in her bedroom to lay comfortable. As Khalia sleeps she begins to toss and turn)

Dream World – Khalia-

As I see myself running in a red dress, with a red bow in my head. I notice nothing but trees and grass and the sounds of birds singing. Hey! Mr. Bee get off my grandmoma's basket, these is my peaches for grandma o make me a peach pie. As I ran to grandma's house, Knock! Knock! Knock! Com e in! as I entered.

Khalia: oh grandma I almost got lost

Grandma: no, not my little baby girl

(as Khalia notice the slop running down grandma's mouth)

Khalia: grandma slops running all out your mouth and its trying to hit my peaches, here's a napkin oh!

(Khalia said as she reach to hand grandma a napkin to wipe her mouth while grandma layed)

Khalia: Grandma!

Grandma: Yes

Khalia: What big teeth you have

Grandma: Mum---- as she looks Khalia in her face

Khalia: Oh what big eyes you have grandma

(as grandma begins to rise up)

Grandma: there better to see you with

Khalia: Grandma

Grandma: Yes

Khalia: and you got a big long tail

(As Khalia screams in fright Moma! Daddy! Mommy! Dad!)

Mom: Khalia

(as Khlia awakes holding on to Mom as tight as she could)

Mom: Khalia! What's wrong dear? You had a nightmare

Khalia: Oh yes! Oh yes! It was grandma alright she really scared me moma, she really looks like and alligator to me.

Khalia Looses a new shoe

Where is Khalia's new shoe, as we prepare to go to chucky cheese for a cousin's birthday party, on route 22

Khalia is all dress up in blue and black with her new shoes on.

Mom: let's go kids we wouldn't wanna be late

Kids: see you later cheobokak!

Ruf—ruff-ruff

Mom: with that big old bone in her mouth

(15 minutes later, here's chucky chesee! Yeah! Yelled the kids)

Khalia runs and play in the playroom alone with her brother, cousins and friends.

Later in the day as we begone to have cake and ice cream.

Khalia returns, down I look at her feet.

Mom: Khalia where is your shoe?

Khalia: I don't know

(As Mom and friends search around inside the ball pin where she was playing, there was no sign of her shoe)

Mom: All Khalia, let's go home

(Khalia jump in the back seat of the car and look out the car window sadly all the way home.)

DOG

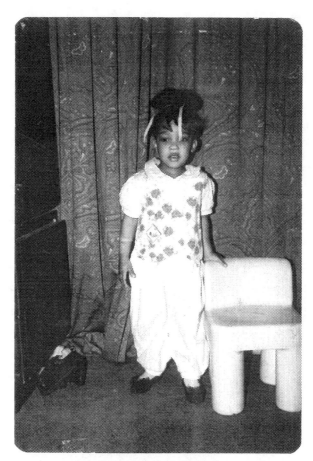

COUSIN JESSICA

Khalia goes to Tampa Florida

Khalia goes to Tampa, Florida and Discover that she might be a weather reporter

(All lined up and ready to go as we pull up in J.F.K 7-24-97, 8: 40 am Flight 261)

Lined up to take off to Tampa, Seat 25A

Khalia gets a window to view the scenery

As she smiles as she buckle up for take off

Khalia: I love you Mom, am Mom says a prayer for take off

Mom: I love you Khalia

(Although the flight Khalia writes and looks around picking up every since of knowledge that she could)

11:30 AM

Pilot: We have just a few minute in arriving to Tampa. Please everyone buckle up and prepare for landing.

Mom: here baby we will be staying at the Day's Inn

Khalia: how far is it

Mom: Just a little while down the road

Mom: oh what a beautiful place Tampa is

7-26-97 Tampa Airport to return to New York City

Khalia- As arriving in Brooklyn

Khalia's friends: Hi Khalia

Khlia: Hey! I discovered some great news

Friends; what's that?

Khalia: don't you know the Map that I always look at in school, it look the same as the one from the window of the plane

Friends: yeah!

Khalia: yes! The same line that's on the map in school is the same line you see as you look out the plane's window

Friends: oj

Khalia: Sure and also, I could tell the weather just like storm field of the news

Friends: wild! Khalia that's something

Khalia: you see as we left New York the weather was rainy when we took off in the air, you could see a full set of clouds over New York and about 45 minutes later you could see partly clouds later then that in some areas you could see lots of sun

Friends: khalia lets play weather reporter just like Stormfield

Khalia: ok some of you who will be living in Florida will have to wear sundresses, cause it was clear there and hot. Next some of you who would like to live in New York needs umbrella cause of the rain fall. And finally but lastsome of you would have to be prepared just in case.

Friends: just in case

Khalia: yeah just in case it rain or the sun shine

Sharif: now let me start with the weather. We have a full set of snow, so put on you a warm coat and your boots and gloves

Friends: Sharif!

Sharif: yes

Friends: where are you

Sharif: Well just about now I am in Alaska

Friends: Alaska! Why Alaska! It's cold there

Sharif: I don't know

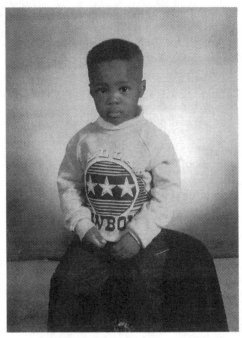

SHARIF

Friend; well wont you hurry up and come back to New York or one of them

Sharif: I don't feel like it right now

Khalia: Boy! Sharif

Well then how we gonna play, dpont nobody have on boots

Sharif: well I guess you figure that one out

Khalia and Friends: we quit Sharif!

You always being smart, come on it's time for us to go in the house now. See you later Khalia.

Khalia: See you all tomorrow.

Wishing you a
Merry Christmas

Baby

By: Annette Fluker

Intro: My baby is coming home to me

My baby is coming home

My baby is coming home to me

(Oh yeah!)

She's coming home

Bridge: there be lots of candy and cookies to eat

(2 times repeat)

Verse: My baby is coming home

Bridge: you can run around and play with me

(3x repeat)

Verse: My baby is coming home

Bridge: you can ride around the world with me

(3x repeat)

(oh yeah!)

She's coming home

Bridge: lots of beauty, water, birds and trees

(3x repeat)

(oh yeah!)

She's coming home!

Merry Christmas

By: Annette Fluker

1st verse: Starlight! Shine so bright

Tell me Jesus, Christ is

2nd verse: charming charms, I fill closer/ closer my dear

3rd verse: twinkle! Twinkle lights that's so clear

4th verse: hold on! Hold on he's here. Starlight's on me_____ even you-----

Choir: Jolly Jolly are we_____ the son in born you see

Choir: for it's Christmas in me Christmas in you, we see, Merry Christmas_ t you

M.E.R.R.Y. Christmas to you

Merry Christmas to you

Choir: M.E.R.R.Y Christmas to you

Merry G Christmas to you F.R.O.M Me!

5th verse: dazzling angel appear

The son is born you see

For its Christmas in me

Christmas in you_ we see

Merry Christmas to you

A Merry Christmas to you

From me---------

The Squirrel that lived in the window

That stupid girl! Yeah Weeboop muttered, why you say hello to them. Whenever anybody say hello to me, I always say hello back. I don't know I can't help it, it's like when someone says thank you, I always say you're welcome back. Don't you automatically say you're welcome? No why. Cause I don't like girls, I rather focus on being a basketball star or even adventure wildlife, what is you gigglen at, nothing let's just focus on getting the others, so we can make it to the picnic. Wooh! Did you see how fast he was driving. Hey Luke! Hey Luke! Hey Luke! Yeal! I'll be right down, in a second. Hey Luke, how was it at the boy's club yesterday, same old same. I tried to make it there, but I couldn't. I hope it don't rain today. Last year it was real nice, we won the tennis match. I show hope that they have the same spot That they had last year, man we got lost and bebop even slip and fell in the lake. It took over and hour before his clothing even dried. Still we had a good time. What's the skate board for Jazz! Whatever, hey! Luke, meme should be coming up this summer. Each year they make it on time for the picnic. It's hot but the breeze feel nice, did you see Charlene It's all most time to have our Tennis match, their she is sitting under the tree eating chips. Hey guys I thought you all wasn't gonna make it. I sure hope they sine this year. I'm going to skating for awhile them I'm going to have me something to at, see you later Charlene. You'll not playing in the match this year, no, I think I'll just sit here and relax, I might even go fishing a little later. Look Charlene look at Luke, with him on the team I just know that they are going to win.

While! Look at how he hit that ball! I'm going to get me something to eat, make sure you taste the salad it's really good, and bring me a soda back please. Here you go, no hot dog, no. I just had one last night. This taste so good I wonder who fix it. I don't know maybe it was lora she always bring salad each year. How far did they get in the game. It looks like Luke's team is winning, look at the Beebop while that's some game. Oh boy! They're playing my song.

Charlene, you can really sing. Come on Cliff let's move a little closer so we can see him sing.

Charlene girl you was singing right with him, what's up Luke where's Weeboop here he comes. We won the game, who's that singing. He wasn't here last year. Get down Charlene, oh look at Weebop man you know you can dance, while! I had to stop skating, a party going on. I'm just moving to the beat. This is some picnic oh yeah, I even see meme to hey Luke what kind of dance is that you're doing. Come on Yazz let's get down. Jazz! Come over here and get you something to eat, you been skating all day. Charlene what you doing back here. I'm tired, here comes Cliff, I'm going fishing before it get too late, I need me a towel to wipe off some of this sweat. Coming Luke, no Cliff, Beebop ho about a little fishing before it get too late. No Cliff, I think I'm just going to eat and relax awhile. Ok see you guys later. So Luke how about asking the fellows to have a ping-pong game at the club next week. Beebop I was thinking the same thing. That was some game ha. Yeah man, I thought we was going to lose when Whalden got to hit the ball. It look as in if it was head over the fence, but he leap up at it our of nowhere and scored. How about that but we still won.

Hey Luke! Maybe we can have some sort of trophy given to the winners. Jazz, let my chair back a little will thanks, Weeboop man I'm really enjoying this day. Lets jam still at Charlene, yeah girl I mean he can sing, Jazz how you like my shades. There nice, let me make sure that I put these cans in the right pan. They has to stay separated for recycle, you know we all have to pitch in and give a hand if we want to continue with this picnic each year. I just love the smell of food being cook on a grill. The city pretty much keep this park well kept up. The grills are new and much larger. That's what I like about it. All you have to do is bring a cooler and some ice alone with your food, the tables and chairs are already here. What time is it Charlene, five thirty five, we still has plenty of time left.

I guess we will be leaving around eight. I won't be skating anymore today I kinda skated out. I normally skate on a daily basis. It's good for your muscles, if I'm not skating, I'm watering flower or even climbing in trees getting apples and oranges. You don't do drill teaming anymore. No, we stop doing all that stuff last year stop I still I kinda miss drilling, all the gilrs on the block would go to other neighborhood's and Challenge, that was lots of fun it didn't matter if we had a uniform or not we offend would wear brown and gold, brown shoe and gold top or gold shorts and a brown top with white sneakers and matching socks and pompoms, a lot of the older neighbor's love to watch us.

They always compliment us and cheer. Jazz on my block we get together and sing. It's four of us in a group we make up dance step tp go alone with the songs. We do it mostly on Saturdays, you should do by some time. I will, I would only have to catch one bus to get to your house right; yeah. Look you guys, have a look at this isn't this something, I really didn't know that I was gonna luck up this good. What kinda fish is that one, a croak fish can't you hear it croke. I see that they have plenty of fish in there. It seems to me like and if I caught enough to last to my next birthday. I even have enough to sort some out. I'm very pleased with this fishing pole I caught on sale, it does a good job, when it comes to fishing it is always good to have fresh bait, this way you get to catch fish more faster. Luke I've been meaning to tell you how much I adore your new apartment maybe you should come by sometimes Charlene so I can give you a tour. He hallway branches into two, you can enter the din or kitchen either way and the rent ain't bad neither, for a studio there's plenty of room for plants and lots of sunlight too. Yeah a man's hope is his castle regardless of how it is.

Speaking of home I guess we all should be headed back. I don't want to miss my bus either Luke. Yo-Beeboop is everybody ready I'm coming, goodbye Meme see you next year. Goodbye Jazz Beeboop Luke, Charlene and Cliff, I'll be writing you all very soon. Ok gang let's all sing one to go on our way to the bus stop.

See you later Charlene.

Let's see soon as I get home I'm going to get my clothes ready for the boy's club tomorrow. Bet me too, I'm gonna make sure that I get there. Hey Luke! Hi Pop, did you all enjoy yourselves today. Yes we did, it was very crowned too. There was sorts of games and singing too. Cliff even caught a loy of fish, let me see um- croke fish and some spots too. This put me in mind of when I was a young boy, I lived all together in a house with a big wraparound porch. Me my mama and daddy and my great grandfather Mr. Jake S. Scott. The S. stood for strong. He was about eighty some years old, we used to sit out on the porch in good weather and he would tell me stories about when he was a boy and the different things that use to happened when he went deep sea fishing. Oh! I loved it so, I loved him so. Tee, he would call me sweet baby tee, some of my favorite stories were his favorites too. Oh how we both loved telling and hearing about the lucky fish. Boy that smile you got remind me of a man a long long long time ago. This man name was Jerome and he loved with his mama right down the road from me and mine. Jerome and his mama use to sit on our front porch.

Just a rockin and snilin, just like you so big and polite, but we was all scared of them because they had, big long teeth and real long finger nail's on their fingers and long toe nails on their toes. They never did say nothing to us, not one word. Till one day me and my friends was passing by them soft like. They was smiling and rocking on the porch and the one Jerome leaned across the banister and whispered right to me with a yellow bandanna wrap around his head. Boy bring me a glass of cool water, I'll give you a lucky fish. Now you know that scared me half to death and dog if I didn't run inside and get pop, Luke Weeboop, Cliff, Jazz.

The coldest glass of water, I can still hear them big teeth knocking on the glass and them long finger nails slickin the glass while he drank it all down his throat. Then he made me come close to him and he reach in this big old pail and handed me a fish. It was one of the biggest fish I had ever seen, I could hardly hold it in my hands. Thank you sir, but that's all right I said to him, but he came to me close as can be right to the banister, take it I have nothing else to offer it's a lucky fish, he said. So I took it and let it go back out to sea, till this day old pop has been one very lucky man. That OK Cliff you did just good. The one I had was too big even try to eat. After all if a fish has live tha long and got that big it just don't make since to mess with it. Now get along its getting late. See you pop, take care. Pop always been very friendly and helpful, right Luke, right Jazz, see you later Jazz, later guys.

Weeboop let's stop at the store. Right Luke, now let's see Weeboop, Cliff what will you have I'll treat. I'll have a bag of chips Luke. Weeboop I'll have a you know, what a mound, no a you know what a snickers no Luke a you know, man boop I'm gonna ask you for the last time, what in the world do you want. Man Luke I said a you know. I don't know nothing, man Luke the candy bar that's the name of it. Oh! Excuse me, what kind of name is that for a candy bar. That was really really funny, let's go. Here's your candy Weeboop. Boop I can't stop laughing that was so funny. I guess I'll be seeing you guys tomorrow right cliff later. See you Luke, Later Weeboop watch yourself Luke going home, yeah I'll call you Weeboop once I get in.

RUFF_RUFF_RUFF_ come on dog, not tonight. Oh boy! Here he comes.

RUFF_RUFF_RUFF_on no! get, get out of here. Whoo--- where am I.

Maybe I can climb this fence, yeah, ok, it might work.

I'm sure glad to be out of that. Hello Beeboop.

I made it home only after running three blocks from that darn dog.

I even had to climb a fence to get away from him

Are you ok, yeah I guess so, see you tomorrow right.

Hey Luke! Hey Luke! Hey Luke! Yeah! I'll be right down.

What's up Weeboop, same old same. Jazz! Where you going with that skate board. All whatever!